M000158276

The
Universal Phrase Book
A Picture Dictionary for International Travelers

The
Universal Phrase Book

A Picture Dictionary for International Travelers

Sterling Publishing Co., Inc.
New York

Produced in 2005 by
PRC Publishing
The Chrysalis Building
Bramley Road, London W10 6SP

An imprint of **Chrysalis** Books Group plc

This edition published in 2005
Distributed in the U.S. and Canada by:
Sterling Publishing Co., Inc.
387 Park Avenue South
New York, NY 10016

© 2005 PRC Publishing

All rights reserved. No part of this publication may
be reproduced, stored in a retrieval system, or transmitted
in any form or by any means, electronic, mechanical,
photocopying, recording, or otherwise, without the prior
written permission of the Publisher and copyright holders.

ISBN 1 4027 2496 9

Printed and bound in Malaysia

All illustrations © Chrysalis Image Library / Mark Franklin.

Contents

Introduction

introduction, introduction, introduction, introduction, introduction,
introduction, introduction, introduction, introduction, introduction,
introduction, introduction, introduction, introduction, introduction,
introduction, introduction, introduction, introduction, introduction,
tion, introduction, introduction,
introduction, introduction, introduction, introduction, introduction,
introduction, introduction, introduction, introduction, introduction,
introduction, introduction, introduction, introduction, introduction,

Worldwide travel used to be the domain of the rich and famous, but better global communication and the growing popularity of low-cost flights means that foreign travel has become available to everyone— from hard-up students to retired couples looking to enjoy their twilight years. However, despite the increase in foreign travel, most Westerners can still speak only one or two languages at best, and generally rely on phrase books or sign language to make themselves understood. With so many far-flung destinations to visit, and the increasing popularity of cruises where a number of countries are visited in a short period of time, most travelers don't have the time to learn the simplest of phrases before they go.

This is where *The Universal Phrase Book* comes in. This guide features a wide range of vocabulary and simple phrases designed to help the traveler in typical situations that they could find themselves in.

Each word is clearly depicted with a simple, representative illustration, allowing the user to point at the image in order to make themselves understood. This all-in-one guide means you don't have to stock up on a variety of different phrase books as this is all you will need to get by.

Divided into useful sections—eating out, places to stay, travel, emergencies, shopping, useful phrases, time, money matters, weather, the post office, social, sightseeing, and numbers—this book will help you communicate when the language barrier proves problematic. Whether you are ordering a meal in China, being examined at the doctors in Prague, or trying to buy some gifts in Egypt, this guide will allow you to get your point across with the minimum of confusion.

Each word is also translated from English into six languages— French, Spanish, German, Italian, Portuguese, and Dutch. These appear alongside each illustration, in the same sequence throughout the book. This means the phrase book can be just as easily used in Brussels and Buenos Aires, as it can be in Burundi or Burkina Faso. Although there can be different dialects within each country, varying from region to region, a pictorial phrase book cuts through the complicated linguistics. Also, there is no need to struggle with a phonetic dictionary—anyone who has attempted a Japanese or Chinese phrase book will enjoy the wonderful simplicity of this approach. Whereas instant cameras are "point and shoot" this system is more like "point and shout."

beer, bière, cerveza,
bier, cerveja, birra,
cocktail, cótet, cock-
tial, coffee, café,
kaffee, koffie, caffè,
milk, lait, leche,

Eating
Out

latte, tea, thé, te, tè,
thee, chá, tè, beer,
bière, cerveza, bier,
cerveja, birra, cock-
tail, cótet, cocktial,
coffee, café, kaffee,
koffie, caffè, milk,
lait, leche, milch,
melk, leite, latte,

restaurant (English)
restaurant (French)
restaurante (Spanish)
Gaststätte (German)
ristorante (Italian)
restaurante (Portuguese)
restaurant (Dutch)

bar (English)
bar (French)
bar (Spanish)
Lokal (German)
bar (Italian)
bar (Portuguese)
bar (Dutch)

cafe (English)
café (French)
café (Spanish)
Kaffee (German)
caffè (Italian)
café (Portuguese)
koffie (Dutch)

Internet cafe
café d'Internet
café de Internet
Internet-Kaffee
caffè del Internet
café do Internet
koffie van Internet

menu
menu
menú
Menü
menu
menu
menu

bill
facture
cuenta
Rechnung
fattura
conta
rekening

vegetarian
végétarien
vegetariano
Vegetarier
vegetariano
vegetariano
vegetariër

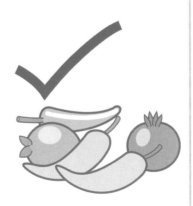

kosher
kascher
aceptable para judíos
koscher
cascer
culinária do judaico
koosjer

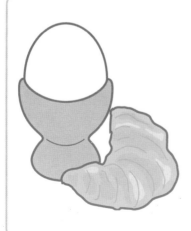

breakfast
petit déjeuner
desayuno
Frühstück
prima colazione
café da manhã
ontbijt

lunch
déjeuner
almuerzo
Mittagessen
pranzo
almoço
lunch

dinner
dîner
cena
Abendessen
cena
jantar
diner

starter
hors-d'oeuvre
primer plato
Vorspeise
antipasti
aperitivo
voorgerecht

main course
plat principal
segundo plato
Hauptgericht
piatto principale
curso principal
hoofd cursus

dessert
dessert
postre
Nachtisch
dessert
sobremesa
dessert

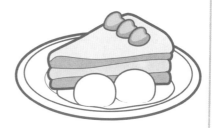

drinks
boissons
bebidas
Getränke
bevande
bebidas
brouwsel

coffee
café
café
Kaffee
caffè
café
koffie

still water
l'eau minéral plat
agua sin gas
Wasser ohne Kohlensäure
acqua naturale
água mineral plana
water niet-gazeus

sparkling water
l'eau minéral gazeuse
agua con gas
Wasser mit Kohlensäure
acqua gasata
água mineral gasosa
water gazeus

milk
lait
leche
Milch
latte
leite
melk

cream
crème
crema
Creme
crema
creme
room

sugar
sucre
azúcar
Zucker
zucchero
açúcar
suiker

milkshake
milk-shake
batido
Milchshake
frullato di latte
batida
milkshake

lemonade
citronnade
limonada
Limonade
limonata
limonada
limonade

orange juice
jus d'orange
jugo de naranja
Orangensaft
succo d'arancia
suco de laranja
sinaasappelsap

cocktail
cocktail
coctel
Cocktail
cocktail
coquetel
cocktail

beer
bière
cerveza
Bier
birra
cerveja
bier

wine
vin
vino
Wein
vino
vinho
wijn

red wine
vin rouge
vino tinto
Rotwein
vino rosso
vinho vermelho
rode wijn

white wine
vin blanc
vino blanco
Weißwein
vino bianco
vinho branco
witte wijn

rosé wine
vin rosé
vino rosé
Roséwein
vino rosé
vinho rosé
rosé wijn

jelly / jam
confiture
mermelada
Marmelade
marmellata
compota
jam

marmalade
confiture d'oranges
mermelada
Marmelade
marmellata d'arance
marmelada
marmelade

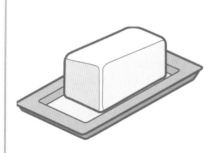

butter
beurre
mantequilla
Butter
burro
manteiga
boter

salt
sel
sal
Salz
sale
sal
zout

pepper
poivre
pimienta
Pfeffer
pepe
pimenta
peper

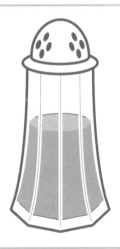

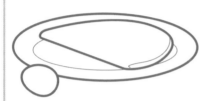

omelette
omelette
tortilla de huevos
Omelett
frittata
omelete
omelet

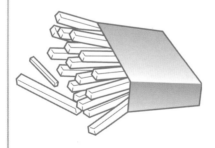

fries / chips
pommes frites
patatas fritas
Pommes frites
patatine fritte
batatas fritas
friet

toast
pain grillé
tostadas
Toast
pane tostato
torrada
toost

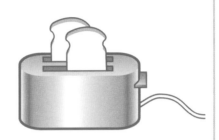

beef
boeuf
carne de vaca
Rindfleisch
manzo
carne
rundvlees

chicken
poulet
pollo
Huhn
pollo
frango
kip

bacon
bacon
tocino
Schinkenspeck
pancetta
bacon
spek

ham
jambon
jamón
Schinken
prosciutto
presunto
ham

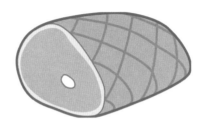

pork
porc
carne de cerdo
Schweinefleisch
maiale
carne de porco
varkensvlees

lamb
agneau
cordero
Lamm
agnello
cordeiro
lamsvlees

salmon
saumon
salmón
Lachs
salmone
salmõe
zalm

tuna
thon
atún
Thunfisch
tonno
atum
tonijn

lobster
langoustine
langosta
Hummer
aragosta
lagosta
zeekreeft

crab
crabe
cangrejo
Krabbe
granchio
caranguejo
krab

oysters
huîtres
ostras
Austern
ostriche
ostras
oesters

sausage
saucisse
salchicha
Wurst
salsiccia
salsicha
worst

burger
hamburger
hamburguesa
Burger
hamburger
hamburguer
hamburger

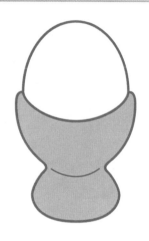

boiled eggs
oeufs à la coque
huevo cocido
weichgekochtes Ei
uovo sodo
ovos quentes
gekookte eieren

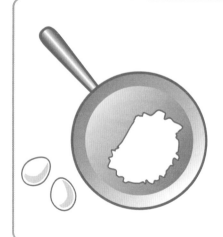

scrambled eggs
oeufs brouillés
huevos revueltos
Rühreier
uova strapazzate
ovos mexidos
roereieren

fried eggs
oeufs sur la plat
huevo frito
Spiegeleier
uovo fritto
ovos fritos
gebrakken eieren

cheese
fromage
queso
Käse
formaggio
queijo
kaas

chips / crisps
chips
patatas fritas
Chipsletten
patatine
batatas fritas
chips

cereal
céréale
cereales
Getreide
cereali
cereal
graangewas

bread
pain
pan
Brot
pane
pão
brood

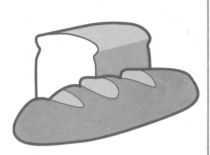

rice
riz
arroz
Reis
riso
arroz
rijst

noodles
nouilles
tallarines
Nudeln
tagliatelle
talharim
noedels

potato
pomme de terre
patata
Kartoffel
patata
batata
aardappel

pizza
pizza
pizza
Pizza
pizza
pizza
pizza

pasta
pâtes
pasta
Teigwaren
pasta
massa
pasta

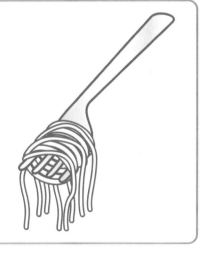

soup
potage
sopa
Suppe
minestra
sopa
soep

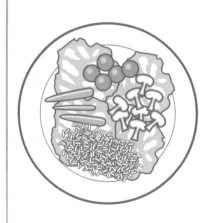

salad
salade
ensalada
Salat
insalata
salada
salade

tomatoes
tomates
tomates
Tomaten
pomodori
tomates
tomaten

sandwich
sandwich
bocadillo
Sandwich
panino
sanduíche
broodje

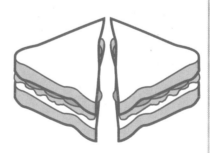

ice cream
glace
helado
Eiscreme
gelato
gelado
ijsje

yogurt
yaourt
yogur
Joghurt
yogurt
iogurte
yoghurt

vegetables
légumes
verdura
Gemüse
verdura
verdura
groenten

onion
oignon
cebolla
Zwiebel
cipolla
cebola
ui

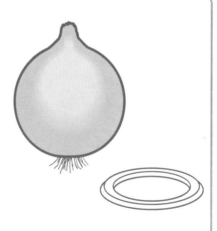

mushrooms
champignons
setas
Pilze
funghi
cogumelos
paddestoelen

fruit
fruit
fruta
Frucht
frutta
fruta
vrucht

strawberries
fraises
fresas
Erdbeeren
fragole
morango
aardbeien

orange
orange
naranja
Orange
arancia
alaranjado
sinaasappel

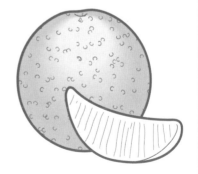

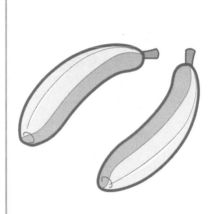

bananas
bananes
plátanos
Bananen
bananes
bananas
banaan

apples
pommes
manzanas
Äpfel
mele
maçãs
appelen

lemon
citron
limón
Zitronen
limoni
limões
citroenen

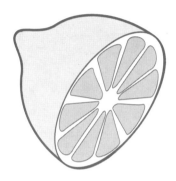

melon
melon
melón
Melone
melone
melão
meloen

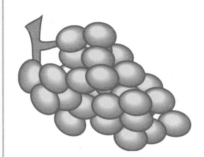

grapes
raisins
uvas
Trauben
uva
uvas
druiven

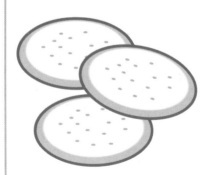

cookies / biscuits
biscuits
galletas
Keks
biscotti
biscoitos
koekjes

cake
gâteau
pastel
Kuchen
torta
bolo
cake

chocolate
chocolat
chocolate
Schokolade
cioccolato
chocolate
chocolade

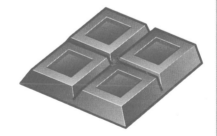

bowl
bol
bol
Schüssel
ciotola
tigela
kom

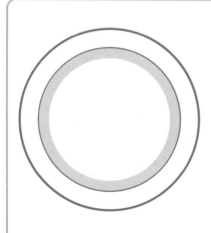

plate
plat
plato
Platte
piatto
placa
bord

glass
verre
vaso
Glas
bicchiere
vidro
glas

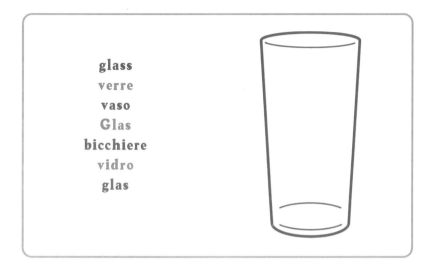

cup
tasse
taza
Tasse
tazza
copo
kopje

knife
couteau
cuchillo
Messer
coltello
faca
mes

fork
fourchette
tenedor
Gabel
forchetta
garfo
vork

spoon
cuillère
cuchara
Löffel
cucchiaio
colher
lepel

ashtray
cendrier
cenicero
Aschenbecher
portacenere
cinzeiro
asbakje

Places to Stay

youth hostel, hotel, bed and breakfast, luggage, vacancies, reservation, confirmation, room service, laundry, tariff, full board, excluding meals, checking out, telephone operator, internet access, fax, messages, safety deposit box, floor, key, room number, towel, pillow, bedding, blanket,

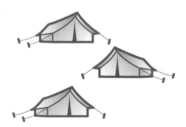

campsite (English)
terrain de camping (French)
camping (Spanish)
Campingplatz (German)
campeggio (Italian)
parque de campismo (Portuguese)
kampeerplaats (Dutch)

tent (English)
tente (French)
tienda (Spanish)
Zelt (German)
tenda (Italian)
tenda (Portuguese)
tent (Dutch)

fire (English)
feu (French)
fuego (Spanish)
Feuer (German)
fuoco (Italian)
fogo (Portuguese)
brand (Dutch)

drinking water
eau potable
agua potable
Trinkwasser
acqua potabile
água potável
drinkwater

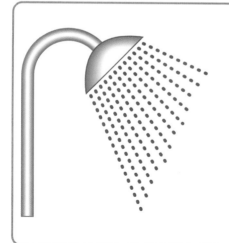

showers
douches
duchas
Duschen
docce
chuveiros
douches

toilets
lavabos
servicios
Toiletten
gabinetti
toaletes
toilet

farm
ferme
granja
Bauernhof
fattoria
quinta
boerderij

torch
lampe de poche
linterna
Taschenlampe
lampadina tascabile
lanterna
zaklantaarn

sleeping bag
sac de couchage
saco de dormir
Schlafsack
sacco a pelo
saco de dormir
slaapzak

youth hostel
l'auberge de jeunesse
albergue juvenil
Jugendherberge
l'ostello della gioventù
pousada da juventude
jeugdherberg

bed and breakfast
pension
pensión
Pension
pensione
pensão
pension

hotel
hôtel
hotel
Hotel
hotel
hotel
hotel

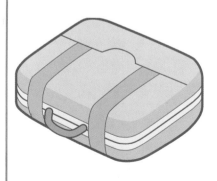

baggage / luggage
bagage
equipaje
Gepäck
bagaglio
bagagem
bagage

vacancies
chambre à louer
habitaciones disponibles
freie Zimmer
posti vacanti
vacâncias
vacatures

reservation
réservation
reservación
Reservierung
prenotazione
reserva
reserve

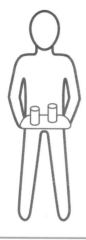

room service
service des chambres
camarero
Zimmerservice
servizio nella stanza
serviço de quarto
ruimte dienst

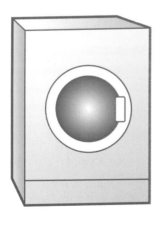

laundry
blanchisserie
lavandería
Wäscherei
lavanderia
lavanderia
wasserij

tariff
tarif
tarifa
Tarif
tariffa
tarifa
tarief

tariff per person
tariff par personne
tarifa por persona
Tarif pro Person
tariffa a persona
tarifa por a pessoa
tarief per persoon

tariff per night
tarif par nuit
tarifa por noche
Tarif pro Nacht
tariffa alla notte
tarifa por a noite
tarief per nacht

tariff per week
tarif par semaine
tarifa por semana
Tarif pro Woche
tariffa alla settimana
tarifa por a semana
tarief per week

full board
pension complète
pensión completa
Vollpension
pensione completa
pensão completa
volpension

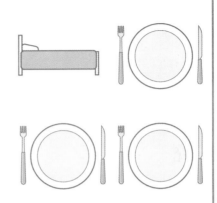

half board
demi-pension
media pensión
Halbpension
mezza pensione
meia-pensão
halfpension

excluding meals
à l'exclusion des repas
excepto comidas
außer Essen
pasti esclusi
sem refeiçãoes
exclusief maaltijd

telephone
téléphone
teléfono
Telefon
telefono
telefone
telefoon

operator
opérateur
operadora
Telephonist
operatore
operador
operator

telephone directory
annuaire du téléphone
guia de teléfonos
Telefonbuch
elenco telefonico
lista telefonica
telefoon boek

telephone number
numéro de téléphone
número de teléfono
Telefonnummer
numero di telefono
número de telefone
telefoonnummer

phonecard
carte de téléphone
tarjeta telefónica
Telefonkarte
scheda del telefono
cartão do telefone
telefoon kaart

Internet access
accès d'Internet
acceso a Internet
Internet-Zugriff
accesso del Internet
acesso do Internet
Internet toegang

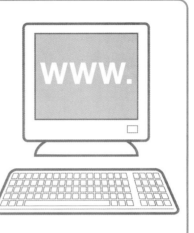

fax
fax
fax
telefax
fax
fax
fax

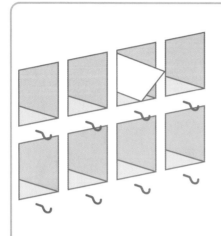

messages
messages
recado
Nachricht
messaggi
mensagem
boodschappen

safety deposit box
coffre-fort
caja de seguridad
Banksafe
cassaforte
cofre
safe

ground floor
rez-de-chaussée
planta baja
Erdgeschoß
pianterreno
rés-do-chão
begane grond

first floor
premier étage
primera planta
erster Stock
primo piano
primeiro andar
eerste verdieping

second floor
deuxième étage
segundo piso
zweiten Stock
secondo piano
segundo andar
tweede verdieping

key
clef
llave
Schlüssel
chiave
chave
sleutel

room number
nombre de chambre
número de habitación
Zimmernummer
numero della stanza
número de quarto
kamer nummer

single / double
chambre a un lit /
chambre por deux
sencilla / doble
einzelnes / doppel
singola / doppia
individual / dobro
**eenpersoonkamer /
tweepersoonkamer**

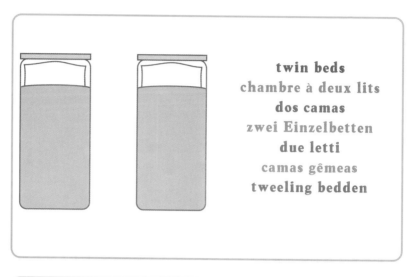

twin beds
chambre à deux lits
dos camas
zwei Einzelbetten
due letti
camas gêmeas
tweeling bedden

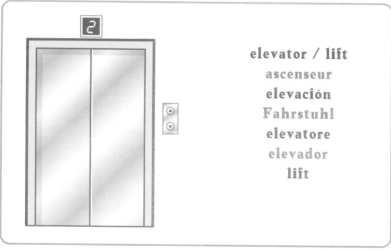

elevator / lift
ascenseur
elevación
Fahrstuhl
elevatore
elevador
lift

smoking
fumer
fumadores
Rauchen
fumare
fumadores
roken

non-smoking
défense de fumer
prohibido fumar
Rauchen verboten
non-fumare
não-fumadores
niet-roken

guest
client
huésped
Gast
ospite
convidado
gast

manager
directeur
director
Manager
direttore
gerente
manager

cleaner
femme de service
camarera
Reinemachefrau
cameriera
empregado da limpeza
kamermeisje

porter
porteur
portero
Portier
facchino
porteiro
portier

maid
femme de chambre
camarera
Zimmermädchen
cameriera
empregada da limpeza
kamermeisje

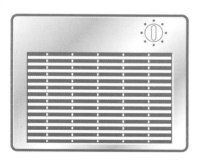

air-conditioning
climatisation
aire acondicionado
Klimatisierung
aria condizionata
ar condicionado
airconditioning

towel
serviette
toalla
Handtuch
asciugamano
toalha
handdoek

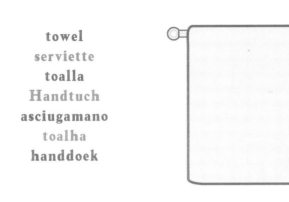

pillow
oreiller
almohada
Kissen
guanciale
almofada
kussen

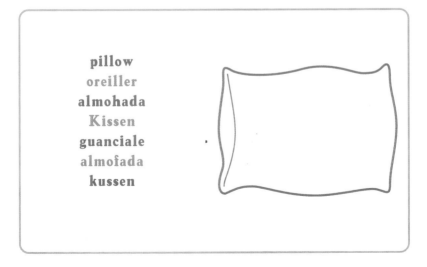

bedding
literie
ropa de cama
Bettzeug
camera da letto
roupa de cama
beddegoed

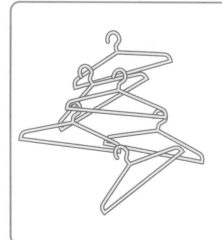

hangers
cintres
perchas
Kleiderbügel
attaccapanni
cabides
klerenhanger

light
lumière
luz
Licht
luce
luz
licht

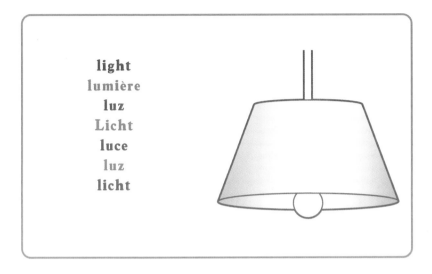

reading lamp
lampe de lecture
lámpara para leer
Leselampe
lampada
candeeiro
lezing lamp

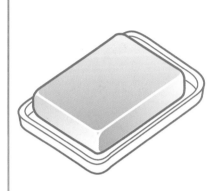

soap
savon
jabón
Seife
saponetta
sabonete
zeep

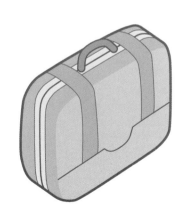

suitcase
valise
maleta
Koffer
valigia
mala de viagem
koffer

bag
sac
bolso
Tasche
sacchetto
saco
tas

backpack / rucksack
sac à dos
mochila
Rucksack
zaino
mochila
rugzak

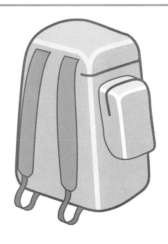

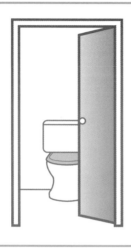

private toilet
toilette privée
retrete privado
Privat-toilette
gabinetto privato
toalete privativos
privé toilet

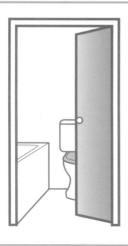

private bathroom
salle de bains privée
cuarto de baño privado
Privat-badezimmer
bagno privato
banheiros privativos
privé badkamers

hot water
eau chaude
agua caliente
Heißwasser
acqua calda
água quente
warm water

bath
bain
baño
Bad
bagno
banho
bad

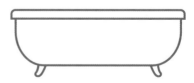

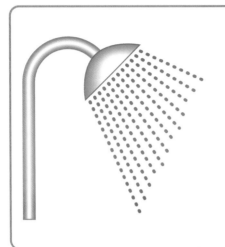

shower
douche
ducha
Dusche
doccia
chuveiro
douche

balcony
balcon
balcón
Balkon
balcone
varanda
balkon

room at the back
derrière l'hôtel
**en la parte
trasera**
Rückseite
camera sul retro
parte traseira
kamer achterkant

sea view
vue de mer
vista al mar
Blick auf das Meer
vista del mare
vista do mar
zee gezicht

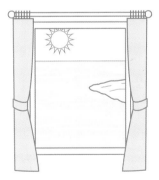

swimming pool
piscine
piscina
Schwimmbad
piscina
piscina
zwembad

quiet room
chambre tranquille
habitación tranquila
ruhig Zimmer
stanza tranquillo
quarto sossegado
rustig kamer

heating
chauffage
calefacción
Heizung
riscaldamento
aquecimento
verwarming

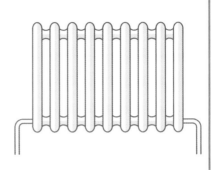

radio
radio
radio
Radio
radio
rádio
radio

television
télévision
televisión
Fernsehen
televisore
televisão
televisie

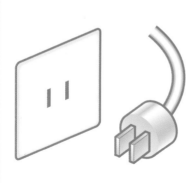

socket
prise de courant
enchufe
Steckdose
presa di corrente
tomada elétrica
stopcontact

iron
fer
plancha
Bugeleisen
ferro
ferro
ijzer

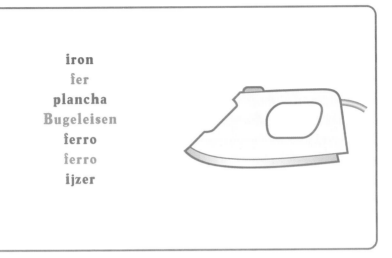

trouser press
presse à patalons
pantalones prensa
Hosenpresse
pantaloni premere
maquina de engomar
as calças
broekpers

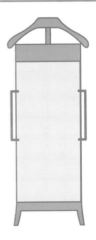

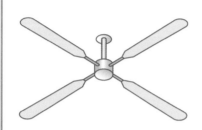

fan
ventilateur
ventilador
Ventilator
ventilatore
ventilador
ventilator

tap
robinet
grifo
Hahn
rubinetto
torneira
kraan

sink
évier
lavabo
Spültisch
catinella
lava-louças
wastafel

blind
store
persiana
Jalousie
persiana
estore
jaloezie

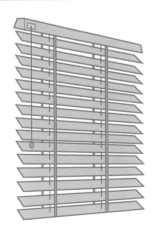

map, ticket, passport, fare, single, return, arrival, departure, first class, second class, economy, travel insurance, baggage, railway station, entrance, exit, ticket office, booking office, buffet, lost property office, platform, waiting room, seat, no smoking carriage, smoking carriage, porter, luggage lockers, taxi

Travel

map (English)
carte (French)
mapa (Spanish)
Landkarte (German)
carta geografica (Italian)
mapa (Portuguese)
kaart (Dutch)

arrival (English)
arrivée (French)
llegada (Spanish)
Ankunft (German)
arrivo (Italian)
chegada (Portuguese)
aankomst (Dutch)

departure (English)
départ (French)
salida (Spanish)
Abflug (German)
partenza (Italian)
partida (Portuguese)
vertrek (Dutch)

ticket
billet
boleto
Karte
biglietto
bilhete
kaartje

passport
passeport
pasaporte
Paß
passaporto
passaporte
paspoort

single
simple
ida
einfach
andata
ida
enkel

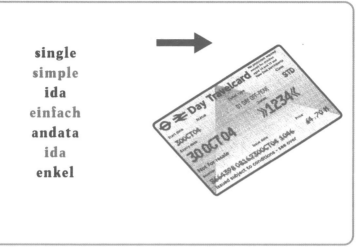

return
retour
ida y vuelta
Rückkehr
andata e ritorno
ida e volta
retour

1st

first class
première classe
primera clase
erstklassig
prima classe
primeira classe
eerste klasse

2nd

second class
deuxième classe
segunda clase
zweite Klasse
seconda classe
segunda classe
tweede klas

economy
classe touriste
economía clase
Touristenklasse
economia classe
classe economica
"economy class"

travel insurance
assurance voyage
seguro
Versicherung
assicurazione
seguro
verzekering

small car
petite voiture
coche pequeño
kleines Auto
automobile piccolo
carro pequeno
kleine auto

large car
grande voiture
coche grande
großes Auto
automobile grande
carro grande
grote auto

sports car
voiture de sport
coche deportivo
Sportwagen
vettura sportiva
carro de desporto
sportpraatje wagen

mileage
kilomètrage
kilometraje
Meilenzahl
chilometraggio
quilometragem
kilometerteller

driving license
permis de conduire
permiso de conducir
Führerschein
patente
carta de condução
rijbewijs

car insurance
assurance d'auto
seguro de coche
Autoversicherung
assicurazione
seguro
verzekering

road sign
poteau indicateur
señal de tráfico
Straßenverkehrszeichen
segnale
sinais de transito
verkeersbord

traffic light
feu de signalisation
semaforo
Verkehrsampel
semaforo
semaforo
stoplicht

parking
stationnement
estacionamiento
Parken
parcheggio
estacionamento
parkeren

no parking
défense de stationner
estacionamiento prohibido
Parken verboten
divieto di sosta
estacionamento proibido
niet parkeren

speed limit
limitation de vitesse
limitación de velocidad
Geschwindigkeitsbegrenzung
limite di velocità
limite de velocidade
snelheidsgrens

motorway
autoroute
autopista
Autobahn
autostrada
auto-estrada
snelweg

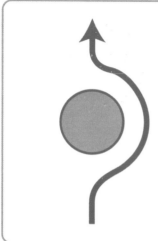

roundabout
rond-point
glorieta
Kreisverkehr
rotonda
rotunda
rotonde

road
route
camino
Straße
strada
estrada
weg

breakdown
panne
coche estropeado
Panne
guasto
avaria
pech

garage
garage
garage
Garage
garage
garagem
garage

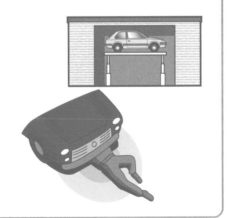

tyre
pneu
neumáticos
Reifen
ruota
pneu
band

ignition key
clef de contact
llaves
Zündschlüssel
chiave
chave
sleutel

fuel gauge
mesure de carburant
indicador de combustible
Benzinuhr
manometro di carburante
mostrador de combustível
brandstof maat

car alarm
alarme de voiture
alarmar del coche
Autoalarm
allarme dell'automobile
alarme do carro
auto alarm

puncture
crevaison
pinchazo
Loch
foratura
furo
platte band

left
gauche
izquierdo
Linke
sinistra
esquerdo
linker

right
droite
derecha
Recht
destra
direita
recht

straight ahead
tout droit
todo derecho
lag direkt
diritto
sempre em frente
rechtdoor

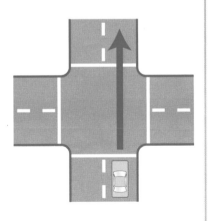

unleaded
sans plomb
sin plomo
bleifrei
senza piombo
sem chumbo
loodvrij

diesel
diesel
gasolina
Diesel
gasolio
gasoleo
diesel

oil
huile
aceite
Öl
olio
óleo
olie

water
eau
agua
Wasser
acqua
água
water

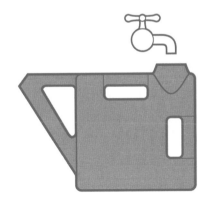

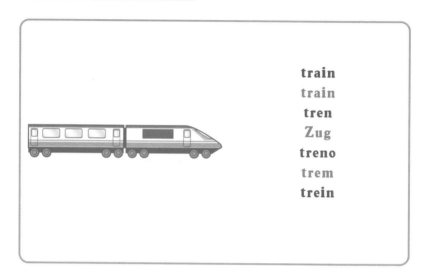

train
train
tren
Zug
treno
trem
trein

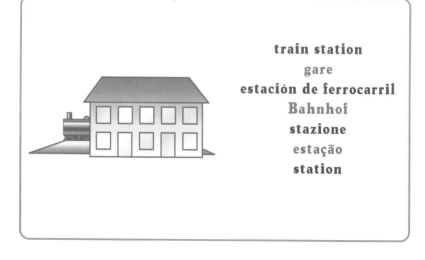

train station
gare
estación de ferrocarril
Bahnhof
stazione
estação
station

entrance
entrée
entrada
Eingang
entrata
entrada
entree

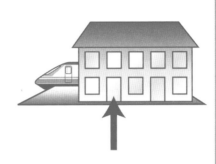

exit
sortie
salida
Ausgang
uscita
saída
uitgang

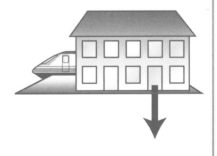

DEPARTURE

ARRIVAL

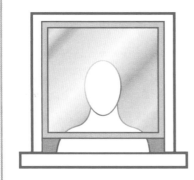

TIMETABLE

timetable
horaire
guia de ferrocarriles
Fahrplan
orario
horário
spoorwegboekje

booking office
bureau de réservation
oficina de reservas
Fahrkartenschalter
ufficio prenotazioni
bilheteira
loket

buffet
buffet
buffet
Speisewagen
buffet
vagão-restaurante
buffet

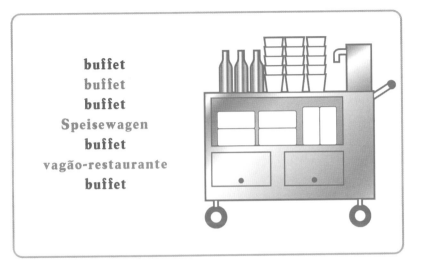

lost property
objets trouvé
oficina de objetos perdidos
Fundbüro
ufficio oggetti smarriti
perdidos e achados
gevonden voorwerpen

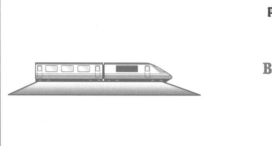

platform
quai
andén
Bahnsteig
binario
linha
perron

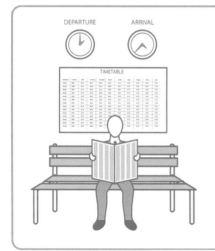

waiting room
salle d'attente
sala de espera
Wartesaal
sala d'aspetto
sala de espera
wachtkamer

taxi
taxi
taxi
Taxi
taxi
táxi
taxi

meter
taximètre
taxímetro
Fahrpreisanzeiger
tassametro
táximetro
taxi meter

plane
avion
plano
Flugzeug
aereo
plano
vliegtuig

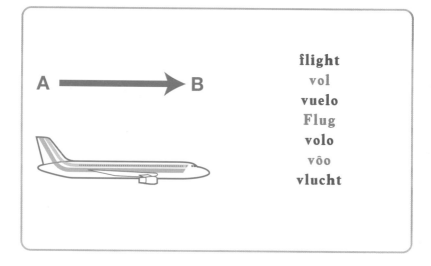

flight
vol
vuelo
Flug
volo
vôo
vlucht

check-in
enregistrement
facturacion
abfertigen lassen
presentarmi
registrar
check-in desk

take-off
décollage
despegue
Start
decollo
decolagem
start

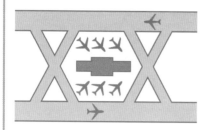

airport
aéroport
aeropuerto
Flughafen
aeroporto
aeroporto
luchthaven

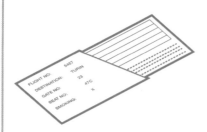

boarding card
carte d'embarquante
tarjeta de embarque
Bordkarte
carta di imbarco
cartão de embarque
boarding-kaart

departure gate
porte d'embarquement
puerta de embarque
Flugsteig
cancello delle partenze
porta de embarque
gate

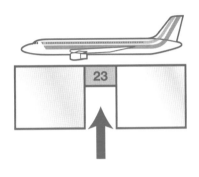

customs
douane
aduana
Zoll
dogana
alfândega
douane

nothing to declare
rien à déclarer
No tengo nada que declarar
nichts zu verzollen
nulla da dichiarare
nada a declarar
niets aan te geven

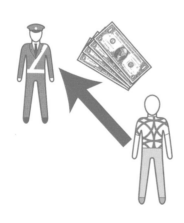

duty
frais de douane
derechos de aduana
Zoll
dazio
taxas aduaneiras
betamelijkheid

ferry
bac
transbordador
Fähre
traghetto
balsa
veerboot

cruise
croisière
travesía
Kreuzfahrt
crociera
cruzeiro
cruise

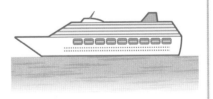

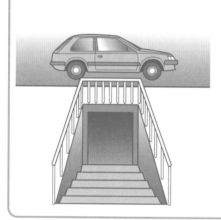

underpass / subway
passage souterrain
paso inferior
Unterführung
sottopassaggio
passagem inferior
tunnel

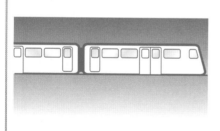

subway / underground
métro
metro
U-Bahn
metropolitana
metro
metro

walking
promenade
paseo
Gehen
camminare
passear
lopen

luggage locker
consigne automatique
**casilleros con llave para
el equipaje**
Gepäckschließfach
custodia dei bagagli
cacifo de bagagem
bagage ministerie

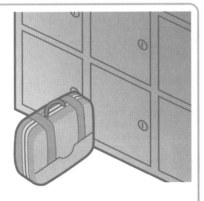

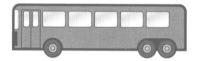

bus
autobus
autobús
Bus
autobus
autocarro
bus

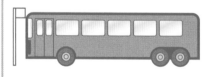

bus stop
arrêt d'autobus
parada de autobúses
Bushaltestelle
fermata dell'autobus
paragem de autocarro
bushalte

coach
autocar
coche
Reisebus
pullman
ônibus
reisbus

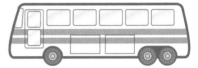

bicycle
bicyclette
bicicleta
Fahrrad
bicicletta
bicicleta
fiets

Help!

doctors, hospital, ambulance, cold, cough, hayfever, upset stomach, headache, sunburn, tablets, medicine, aspirin, cream, band-plasters, con... ...ect repellent, surgery, vaccination, pain, sore throat, nausea, faint, head, stomach, leg, ankle, arm, nose, teeth, hand, foot, face, back, chest

doctor (English)
docteur (French)
doctor (Spanish)
Doktor (German)
medico (Italian)
médico (Portuguese)
dokter (Dutch)

hospital (English)
hôpital (French)
hospital (Spanish)
Krankenhaus (German)
ospedale (Italian)
hospital (Portuguese)
ziekenhuis (Dutch)

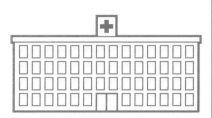

ambulance (English)
ambulance (French)
ambulancia (Spanish)
Krankenwagen (German)
ambulanza (Italian)
ambulância (Portuguese)
ziekenwagen (Dutch)

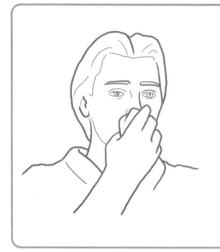

cold
rhume
resfriado
Erkältung
raffreddore
constipação
verkoudheid

cough
toux
tos
Husten
tosse
tosse
hoest

upset stomach
mal de ventre
dolor de estómago
Magenschmerzen
mal di stomaco
dor de estômago
maagpijn

headache
mal à la tête
dolor de cabeza
Kopfschmerzen
mal di testa
dor de cabeça
hoofdpijn

sunburn
coup de soleil
quemaduras del sol
Sonnenbrand
scottatura solare
queimadura de sol
zonnebrand

sore throat
mal de gorge
garganta irritada
Halsschmerzen
mal di gola
dor de garganta
keelpijn

faint
défaillant
desmayar
schwach
stordito
desmaiar
duizelig

nausea
nausée
con náuseas
Übelkeit
nausea
náusea
misselijkheid

hayfever
rhume des foins
fiebre del heno
Heuschnupfen
febbre del fieno
febre dos fenos
hooikoorts

tablets
comprimés
tabletas
Tabletten
pastiglie
tabuletas
tabletten

medicine
médecine
medicina
Medizin
medicina
medicina
geneeskunde

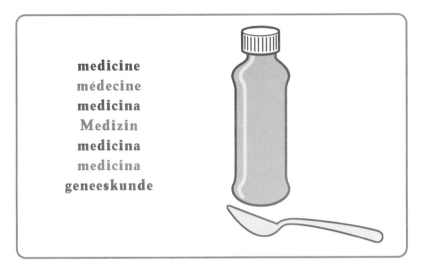

aspirin
aspirine
aspirina
Aspirin
aspirina
aspirina
aspirine

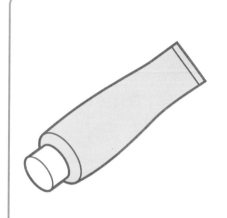

cream (ointment)
onguent
ungüento
Salbe
unguento
lubrificante
saus

bandage
bandage
vendaje
Verband
benda
ligadura
verband

bandaids / plasters
sparadrap
tirita
Pflaster
cerotto
emplastros
pleister

contraception
contraception
contracepción
Empfängnisverhütung
antifecondativo
contraceptivo
voorbehoedsmiddel

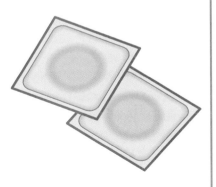

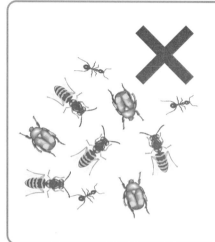

insect repellent
crème anti-insecte
repelente para insectos
Insektenvertreibend
crema contro gli insetti
repelente de insectos
insektenwerend middel

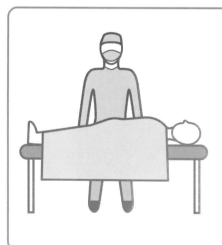

surgery
chirurgie
cirugía
Chirurgie
chirurgia
cirurgia
chirurgie

vaccination
vaccination
vacunación
Schutzimpfung
vaccinazione
vacinação
inenting

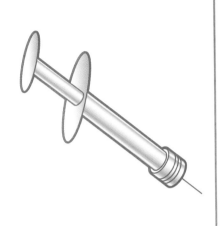

pain
douleur
dolor
Schmerz
dolore
dor
pijn

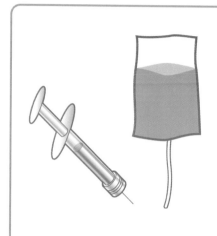

blood
sang
sangre
Blut
sangue
sangue
bloed

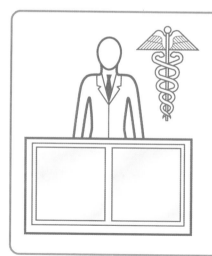

pharmacy
pharmacie
farmacia
Apotheke
farmacia
farmácia
apotheek

dentist
dentiste
dentista
Zahnarzt
dentista
dentista
tandarts

toothache
mal de dents
dolor de muelas
Zahnschmerz
mal di denti
dores de dentes
tandpijn

disabled access
accès pour les handicapés
acceso (inválido)
behindert Zugang
accesso por gli andicappati
acesso para os deficientes
**toegang voor
gehandicapten**

crime
crime
crimen
Verbrechen
crimine
crime
misdaad

police
gendarmerie
policía
Polizei
polizia
polícias
politie

fine
contravention
multa
Geldstrafe
pena
multa
geldboete

help
aide
ayuda
Hilfe
aiuto
ajuda
hulp

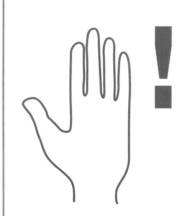

stop
arrêttez
detenga
Halt
fermatevi
agarra
stop

fireman
pompier
bombero
Feuerwehrmann
vigile del fuoco
bombeiro
brandweerman

embassy
ambassade
embajada
Botschaft
ambasciata
embaixada
ambassade

make up, perfume;
gifts, newspapers,
magazines, photogra-
phy, supermarket,
groceries, travel
agent, bookshop, chi-
naware, glassware,
drugstore, florist,

Shopping

jewellers, laundry,
dry cleaners, market,
tobacconist, hair-
dresser, cigar,
cigarette, camera,
camera film, paper,
pen, pencil, battery

jewelry (English)
bijoux (French)
joyería (Spanish)
Schmuck (German)
gioielli (Italian)
jóias (Portuguese)
juwelen (Dutch)

necklace (English)
collier (French)
collar (Spanish)
Halskette (German)
collana (Italian)
colar (Portuguese)
halsketting (Dutch)

bracelet (English)
bracelet (French)
pulsera (Spanish)
Armband (German)
braccialetto (Italian)
pulseira (Portuguese)
armband (Dutch)

ring
anneau
sortija
Ring
anello
anel
ring

earrings
boucles d'oreille
pendientes
Ohrringe
orecchinos
brincos
oorbellen

makeup
maquillage
maquillage
Schminke
trucco
maquilhagem
make-up

perfume
parfum
perfume
Parfüm
profumo
perfume
parfum

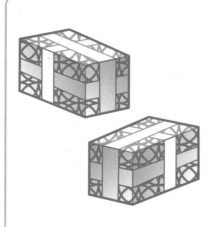

gifts
cadeaux
regalos
Geschenke
regali
presentes
cadeau

newspaper
journal
periódico
Zeitung
giornale
jornal
krant

magazine
magazine
revista
Zeitschrift
revista
revista
tijdschrift

supermarket
supermarché
supermercado
Supermarkt
supermercato
supermercado
supermarkt

groceries
épicerie
tienda de comestibles
Lebensmittel
drogheria
armazém
kruidenierswinkels

travel agent
agent de voyages
agente de viajes
Reisebüro
agente di viaggio
agente de viagens
reisbureau

bookshop
librairie
librería
Buchhandlung
libreria
livraria
boekwinkel

chinaware
porcelaine
porcelana
Porzellan
porcellana
porcelana
porselein

glassware
verrerie
cristalería
Glaswaren
articolo di vetro
artigos de vidro
glaswerk

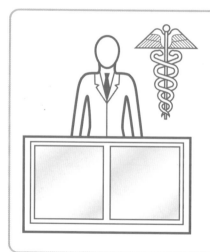

drugstore
pharmacie
farmacia
Drugstore
farmacia
farmacia
drogisterij

florist
fleuriste
floreria
Blumenhändler
fiorista
florista
bloemenwinkel

bakery
boulangerie
panadería
Bäckerei
panetteria
padaria
bakker

jeweler / jeweller
bijoutiers
joyeria
Juweliergeschäft
gioielleria
joalharia
juweliers

laundrette
blanchisserie
lavanderia
Munzwäscherei
lavanderia
lavanderia
wasserette

dry cleaner's
nettoyeurs à sec
tintoreria
chemische Reinigung
lavanderie a secco
lavandaria de limpeza a seco
stomerij

market
marché
mercado
Markt
mercato
mercado
markt

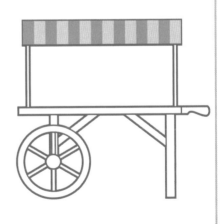

hairdresser
coiffeur
peluquero
Friseur
parrucchiere
cabeleireiro
kapper

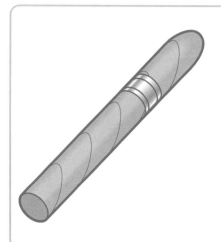

cigar
cigare
puro
Zigarre
sigaro
charuto
sigaar

cigarette
cigarette
cigarrillo
Zigarette
sigaretta
cigarro
sigaret

camera
appareil-photo
cámara fotográfica
Kamera
macchina fotografica
máquina fotográfica
fototoestel

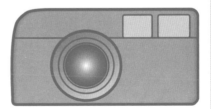

paper
papier
papel
Papier
carta
papel
papier

pen
stylo
pluma
Kugelschreiber
penna
caneta
pen

pencil
crayon
lápiz
Bleistift
matita
lápis
potlood

batteries
piles
pilas
Batterien
pilas
pilhas
batterijen

clock
horloge
reloj
Uhr
orologio
relogio
klok

clothing
habillement
ropa
Kleidung
abbigliamento
roupa
kleding

hat
chapeau
sombrero
Hut
cappello
chapéu
hoed

dress
robe
vestido
Kleid
abito
vestido
jurk

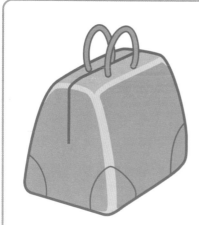

bag
sac
bolso
Beutel
sacchetto
saco
tas

shoes
chaussures
zapatos
Schuhe
scarpe
sapatas
schoenen

jacket
veste
chaqueta
Jacke
giacca
curto
jasje

coat
manteau
abrigo / gaban
Mantel
cappotto
casaco
jas

skirt
jupe
falda
Rock
gonna
saia
rok

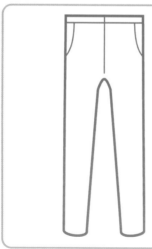

pants / trousers
pantalon
pantalones
Hose
pantaloni
calças
lange broek

belt
ceinture
cinturon
Gürtel
cintura
cinto
riem

shorts
short
pantalones cortos
Shorts
short
calções
korte broek

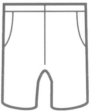

shirt
chemise
camisa
Hemd
camicia
camisa
overhemd

sweater
tricot
suéter
Pullover
maglione
camisola
trui

watch
montre
reloj
Armbanduhr
orologiaio
relógio
horloge

jeans
jeans
tejanos
Jeans
jeans
jeans
jeans

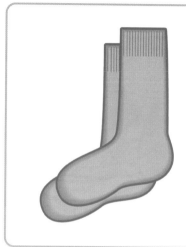

socks
chaussettes
calcetines
Socken
calzini
peuga
sokken

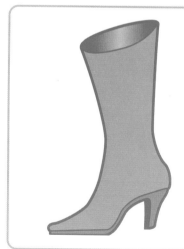

boots
bottes
botas
Stiefel
stivale
botas
laarzen

pyjamas
pyjamas
pijamas
Schlafanzüge
pigiama
pyjamas
pyjama

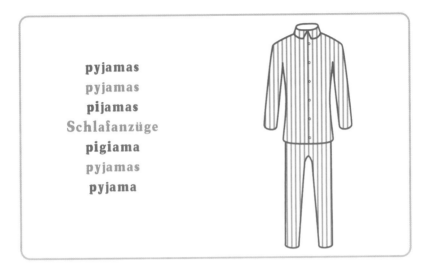

scarf
écharpe
bufanda
Schal
sciarpa
lenço de pescoço
sjaal

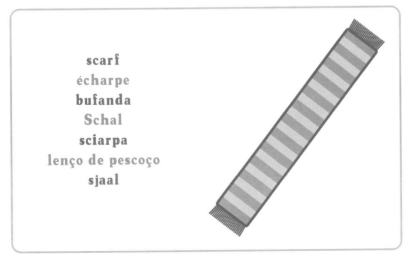

gloves
gants
guantes
Handschuhe
guanti
luvas
handschoenen

SIZE: 12

PRICE: £24.99

size
taille
talla
Größe
taglia
tamanho
maat

changing rooms
vestiaires
probador
Ankleideraum
cabina di prova
vestiàrios
paskamer

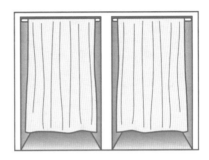

toiletries
articles de toilette
artículos de aseo
Toilettenartikel
articoli da toilette
artigos de higiene
toiletartikelen

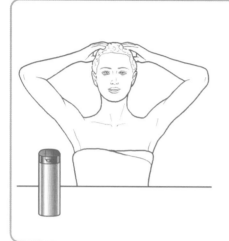

shampoo
shampooing
champú
Shampoo
sciampo
shampoo
shampoo

razor
rasoir
navaja de afeitar
Rasiermesser
rasoio
navalha
scheerapparaat

suncream
lotion solaire
crema solar
Sonnenöl
crema solare
creme debronzear
zonnebrandcreme

tissues
mouchoir en papier
pañuelo de papel
Papiertaschentuch
fazzoletto di carta
lenços de papel
tissue

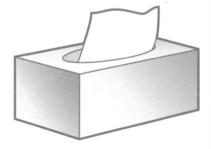

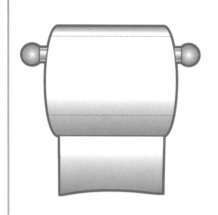

toilet paper
papier hygiénique
papel higiénico
Toilettenpapier
carta igienica
papel higiénico
toiletpapier

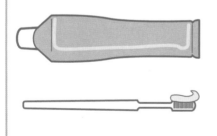

toothpaste
pâte dentifrice
pasta de dientes
Zahnpaste
dentifricio
pasta de dentes
tandpasta

toothbrush
brosse à dents
cepillo de dientes
Zahnbürste
spazzolino da denti
escova de dentes
tandenborstel

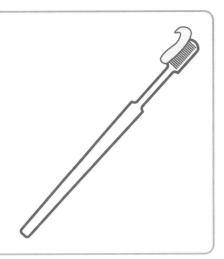

sanitary products
serviette hygiénique
compresas
Damenbinde
assorbente igienico
pensos higiénicos
luiers

hairbrush
brosse de cheveux
cepillo del pelo
Haarbürste
spazzola dei capelli
escova de cabelo
haar borstel

umbrella
parapluie
paraguas
Regenschirm
ombrello
guarda-chuva
paraplu

discount
escompte
descuento
Diskont
sconto
disconto
korting

$5

toys
jouets
juguetes
Spielwaren
giocattoli
brinquedos
speelgoed

Useful Phrases

yes **(English)**
oui **(French)**
sí (Spanish)
ja **(German)**
sì (Italian)
sim **(Portuguese)**
ja (Dutch)

no (English)
non (French)
no (Spanish)
nein (German)
no (Italian)
não (Portuguese)
nee (Dutch)

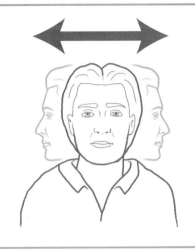

hungry (English)
affamé (French)
hambriento (Spanish)
hungrig (German)
affamato (Italian)
com fome (Portuguese)
hongerig (Dutch)

thirsty
soif
sediento
durstig
sete
com sede
dorstig

tired
fatigué
cansado
müde
stanco
cansado
vermoeid

lost
perdu
perdido
verloren
perduto
perdido
verdwaald

big
grand
grande
groß
grande
grande
groot

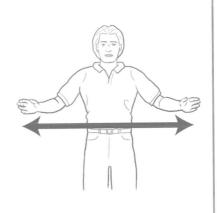

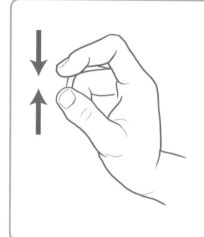

small
petit
pequeño
klein
piccolo
pequeno
klein

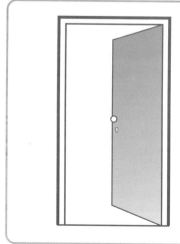

open
ouvert
abierto
geöffnet
aperto
aberto
open

shut
fermé
cerrado
geschlossen
chiuso
fechado
dicht

good
bon
bueno
gut
buono
bom
goed

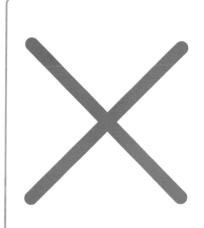

bad
mauvais
malo
schlecht
cattivo
mau
slecht

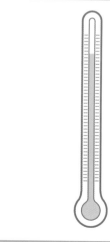

hot
chaud
caliente
heiß
caldo
quente
heet

cold
froid
frío
kalt
freddo
frio
koude

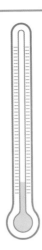

expensive
cher
caro
kostspielig
caro
caro
duur

cheap
bon marché
barato
billig
buon mercato
barato
goedkoop

quiet
tranquille
tranquilidad
still
tranquillo
sossegado
rustig

noisy
bruyant
ruidoso
laut
rumoroso
barulhento
lawaaierig

holiday
vacances
vacación
Urlaub
vacanze
feriado
vakantie

business
affaires
negocio
Geschäft
affari
negócio
zaken

son / daughter
fils / fille
hijo / hija
Sohn / Tochter
figlio / figlia
filho / filha
zoon / dochter

father
père
padre
Vater
padre
pai
vader

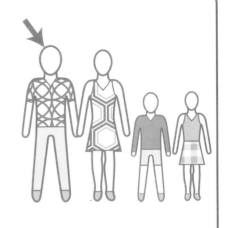

mother
mère
madre
Mutter
madre
mãe
moeder

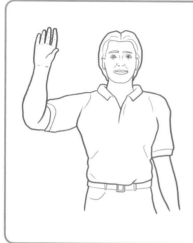

hello
bonjour
hola
hallo
ciao
olá
dag

goodbye
au revoir
adiós
auf Wiedersehen
arrivederci
adeus
dag

man
homme
hombre
Mann
uomo
homem
man

woman
femme
mujer
Frau
donna
mulher
vrouw

Time, Dates, & Seasons

half past, quarter past, quarter to, days of week, monday, tuesday, wednesday, thursday, friday, saturday, sunday, january, february, march, april, may, june, july, august, september, october, november, december, seasons, spring, summer, yesterday, today, tomorrow, year

midday (English)	one o'clock	two o'clock
midi (French)	une heure	deux heures
mediodía (Spanish)	**las uno**	**las dos**
Mittag (German)	ein Uhr	zwei Uhr
mezzogiorno (Italian)	**un in punto**	**due in punto**
meio-dia (Portuguese)	um horas	dois horas
middag (Dutch)	**één uur**	**twee uur**

three o'clock
trois heures
las tres
drei Uhr
tre in punto
três horas
drie uur

four o'clock
quatre heures
las cuatro
vier Uhr
quattro in punto
quatro horas
vier uur

five o'clock
cinq heures
las cinco
fünf Uhr
cinque in punto
cinco horas
vijf uur

six o'clock
six heures
las seises
sechs Uhr
sei in punto
seis horas
zes uur

seven o'clock
sept heures
las siete
sieben Uhr
sette in punto
sete horas
zeven uur

eight o'clock
huit heures
las ocho
acht Uhr
otto in punto
oito horas
acht uur

nine o'clock
neuf heures
las nueve
neun Uhr
nove in punto
nove horas
negen uur

ten o'clock
dix heures
las diez
zehn Uhr
dieci in punto
dez horas
tien uur

eleven o'clock
onze heures
las once
elf Uhr
undici in punto
onze horas
elf uur

midnight
minuit
medianoche
Mitternacht
mezzanotte
meio-noite
middernacht

quarter after / past
et quart
y cuarto
Viertel nach
e un quarto
e um quarto
kwart over

quarter to / of
moins un quart
menos cuarto
Viertel vor
meno un quarto
um quarto para
kwart voor

Monday, lundi, **lunes,** Montag, **lunedì,** segunda-feira, **maandag**

Tuesday, mardi, **martes,** Dienstag, **martedì,** terça-feira, **dinsdag**

Wednesday, mercredi, **miércoles,** Mittwoch, **mercoledì,** quarta-feira, **woensdag**

Thursday, jeudi, **jueves,** Donnerstag, **giovedì,** quinta-feira, **donderdag**

Friday, vendredi, **viernes,** Freitag, **venerdì,** sexta-feira, **vrijdag**

Saturday, samedi, **sábado,** Samstag **sabato,** sábado, **zaterdag**

Sunday, dimanche, **domingo,** Sonntag **domenica,** domingo, **zondag**

spring
printemps
primavera
Frühling
primavera
primavera
de lente

summer
été
verano
Sommer
estate
verão
de zomer

fall / autumn
automne
otoño
Herbst
autunno
outono
de herfst

winter
hiver
invierno
Winter
inverno
inverno
de winter

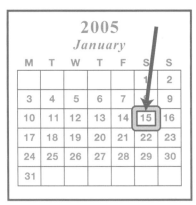

2005
January

M	T	W	T	F	S	S
					1	2
3	4	5	6	7	8	9
10	11	12	13	14	15	16
17	18	19	20	21	22	23
24	25	26	27	28	29	30
31						

yesterday
hier
ayer
gestern
ieri
ontem
gisteren

2005
January

M	T	W	T	F	S	S
					1	2
3	4	5	6	7		9
10	11	12	13	14	15	16
17	18	19	20	21	22	23
24	25	26	27	28	29	30
31						

today
aujourd'hui
hoy
heute
oggi
hoje
vandaag

tomorrow
demain
mañana
morgen
domani
amanhã
morgen

		2005 *January*				
M	T	W	T	F	S	S
					1	2
3	4	5	6	7	8	9
10	11	12	13	14	15	16
17	18	19	20	21	22	23
24	25	26	27	28	29	30
31						

week
semaine
semana
Woche
settimana
semana
week

		2005 *January*				
M	T	W	T	F	S	S
					1	2
3	4	5	6	7	8	9
10	11	12	13	14	15	16
17	18	19	20	21	22	23
24	25	26	27	28	29	30
31						

2005
January

M	T	W	T	F	S	S
					1	2
3	4	5	6	7	8	9
10	11	12	13	14	15	16
17	18	19	20	21	22	23
24	25	26	27	28	29	30
31						

day
jour
día
Tag
giorno
dia
dag

morning
matin
mañana
Morgen
mattina
manhã
morgen

afternoon
après-midi
tarde
Nachmittag
pomeriggio
tarde
middag

evening
soirée
tarde
Abend
sera
noite
avond

Money

bank, currency exchange, travellers' cheques, cheque, credit cards, dollars, sterling, euros, exchange rate, notes, cash, coins, bank statement, cash point exchange, travellers' cheques, cheque, credit cards, dollars, sterling, euros, exchange rate, notes, cash, coins, bank statement, cash

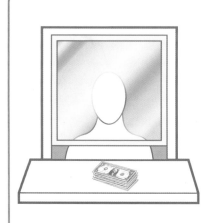

bank (English)
banque (French)
banco (Spanish)
Bank (German)
banca (Italian)
banco (Portuguese)
bank (Dutch)

**currency exchange
(English)**
bureau de change
(French)
**oficina de cambio
(Spanish)**
Wechseln (German)
ufficio cambio (Italian)
bureau de change
(Portuguese)
**geldwisselkantoor
(Dutch)**

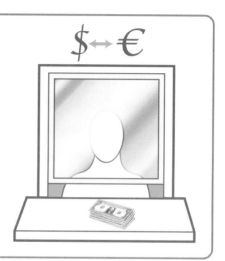

**traveler's checks / cheques
(English)**
chèques de voyage (Fr)
cheques de viajero (Sp)
Reiseschecke (German)
traveller's cheques (It)
cheques de viagens (Port)
reischeque (Dutch)

check / cheque
chèque
cheque
Scheck
assegno
cheque
cheque

credit card
carte de crédit
tarjeta de crédito
Kreditkarte
carta di credito
cartão de crédito
creditcard

dollars
dollars
dólares
Dollar
dollari
dólares
dollars

pound sterling
livre sterling
libra esterlina
Pfund
sterlina
libra
pond

euros
euros
euros
Euro
euro
euros
euro

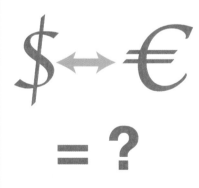

exchange rate
taux de change
cambio
Wechselkurs
corso del cambio
câmbio
wisselkoers

bank notes
billet
billetes
Banknoten
bancanota
cambial
bankbiljet

cash
argent comptant
dinero en efectivo
Kleingeld
contanti
dinheiro
contant geld

coins
pièces de monnaie
monedas
Münzen
monetas
moedas
muntstukken

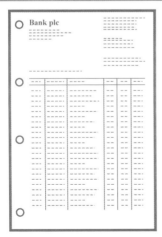

bank statement
relevé de compte
estado de cuentas
Auszug
estratto di conto
extracto de banco
verlies-en winstrekening

ATM / cash dispenser
distributeur de billets
cajero automático
Nachtschalter
punto dei contanti
multibancos
geldautomaat

rain, sun, hot, cold, thunder and lightning, snow, wind, fog, clear, cloudy, temperature, rain, sun, hot, cold, thunder and lightning, snow, wind, fog, clear,

Weather

rain, sun, hot, cold, thunder and lightning, snow, wind, fog, clear, cloudy, temperature, rain, sun, hot, cold, thunder and lightning, snow

rain (English)
pluie (French)
lluvia (Spanish)
Regen (German)
pioggia (Italian)
chover (Portuguese)
regenen (Dutch)

sun (English)
soleil (French)
sol (Spanish)
Sonne (German)
sole (Italian)
sol (Portuguese)
zon (Dutch)

hot (English)
chaud (French)
caliente (Spanish)
heiß (German)
caldo (Italian)
quente (Portuguese)
heet (Dutch)

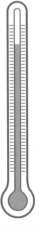

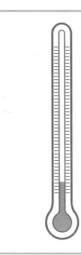

cold
froid
frío
kalt
freddo
frio
koude

thunder
tonnerre
trueno
Donner
tuono
trovão
donder

snow
neige
nevara
Schnee
neve
nevar
sneeuw

wind
vent
viento
Wind
vento
vento
waait

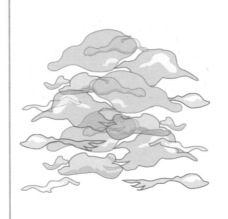

fog
brouillard
niebla
Nebel
nebbia
névoeiro
mistig

clear
clair
cielo despejado
klar
chiaro
claro
klaar

cloudy
nuageux
nublado
bewölkt
nuvoloso
nublado
enevoado

temperature
température
temperatura
Temperatur
temperatura
temperatura
temperatuur

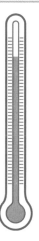

parcel, letter, mail, stamp, postcard, airmail, mailbox, parcel, letter, mail, stamp, postcard, airmail, mailbox, parcel, letter, mail, stamp, postcard, airmail, mailbox, letter, ter, mail, stamp, postcard, airmail, mailbox, parcel, letter, mail, stamp, postcard, airmail, mailbox, parcel, letter, mail, stamp

Post

parcel (English)
colis (French)
paquete (Spanish)
Paket (German)
paccho (Italian)
pacote (Portuguese)
packkje (Dutch)

letter (English)
lettre (French)
carta (Spanish)
Brief (German)
lettera (Italian)
carta (Portuguese)
brief (Dutch)

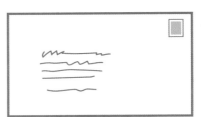

mail (English)
courrier (French)
correo (Spanish)
Post (German)
posta (Italian)
correio (Portuguese)
post (Dutch)

stamp
timbre
sello
Briefmarke
francobollo
selo
postzegel

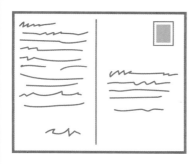

postcard
carte postale
tarjeta
Postkarte
cartolina
postal
kaart

airmail
poste aérienne
correo aéreo
Luftpost
via aerea
via aérea
luchtpost

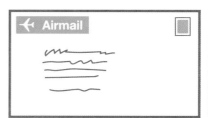

mailbox
boîte aux lettres
buzón
Briefkasten
cassetta delle lettere
postal do correio
brievenbus

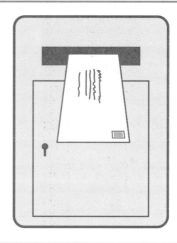

nightclub, dancing,
bar, pub, cinema,
film, tickets, subti-
tles, theatre, play,
opera, ballet, concert,
jazz, pop, classical,
music, skiing, foot-
ball, football match,
g
ning, tennis, fishing,
horse riding, moun-
tain biking, hiking,
beach, party, dinner
party, chatting,
email, friends, cheers,
birthday, tennis

Social

nightclub (English)
boîte de nuit (French)
sala de fiestas (Spanish)
Nachtklub (German)
night-club (Italian)
boate (Portuguese)
nachtclub (Dutch)

bar (English)
bar (French)
bodega (Spanish)
Lokal (German)
bar (Italian)
bar (Portuguese)
bar (Dutch)

pub (English)
pub (French)
taberna (Spanish)
Kneipe (German)
bar (Italian)
cervejaria (Portuguese)
bierhuis (Dutch)

tickets
billets
entradas
Karten
biglietti
bilhetes
kaartjes

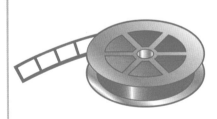

movie / film
film
película
Film
film
filme
film

theater / theatre
théâtre
teatro
Theater
teatro
teatro
theater

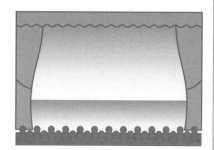

play
pièce de théâtre
obra de teatro
Theaterstück
commedia
peça para teatro
toneelstuk

opera
opéra
ópera
Oper
opera
ópera
opera

ballet
ballet
ballet
Ballett
balletto
bailado
ballet

concert
concert
concierto
Konzert
concerto
concerto
concert

jazz
jazz
jazz
Jazz
jazz
jazz
jazz

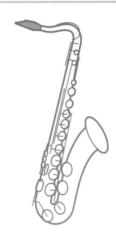

rock
rock
rock
Rock
rock
rock
rock

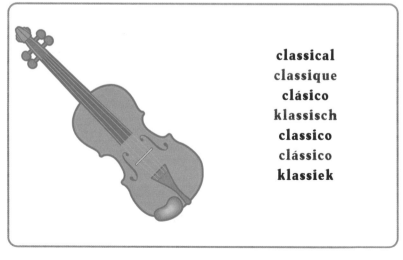

classical
classique
clásico
klassisch
classico
clássico
klassiek

music
musique
música
Musik
musica
música
muziek

skiing
ski
esquí
Skilaufen
sci
esquiar
skisport

soccer / football
football
fútbol
Fußball
calcio
futebol
voetbal

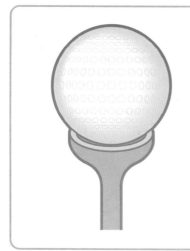

golf
golf
golf
Golf
golf
golfe
golf

swim
natation
natación
Schwimmen
nuoto
natação
zwemmen

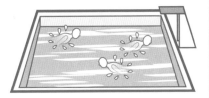

run
courir
correr
Lauf
correre
correr
hardlopen

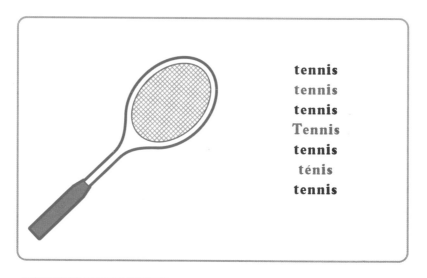

tennis
tennis
tennis
Tennis
tennis
ténis
tennis

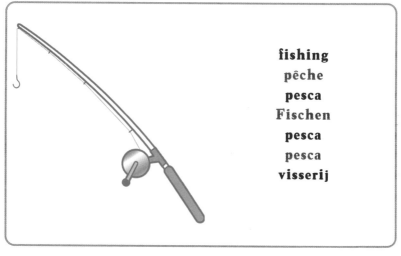

fishing
pêche
pesca
Fischen
pesca
pesca
visserij

horse riding
équitation
equitacion
Pferdereiten
corsa di cavalli
corrida de cavalos
paardrijden

mountain biking
faire de la bicyclette
montando en bicicleta
Radfahren
ciclismo
ciclismo
wielrennen

hiking
excursion
ir de excursión
Wandern
fare un'excursione a piedi
fazer longas caminhadas a pé
wandeling

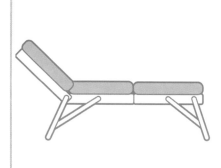

sunlounger
fauteuil bain de soleil
silla de lona
Liegestuhl
sedia a sdraio
uma cadeira de encosto
ligstoel

dinner party
dîner
cena
Abendgesellschaft
cena
jantar em casa
diner feestje

birthday
anniversaire
cumpleaños
Geburtstag
compleanno
aniversário
verjaardag

Sight-seeing

guide book, street map, church, cathedral, museum, art galleries, exhibition, excursions, tour guide, audio guides, ... information centre, castle, gardens, park, lake, temple, market, ... palace, river, tower, zoo, camera, photography, camcorder, tourist information centre, castle

guidebook (English)
guide (French)
guía (Spanish)
Reiseführer (German)
guida turistica (Italian)
guia (Portuguese)
gids (Dutch)

street (English)
rue (French)
calle (Spanish)
Straße (German)
via (Italian)
rua (Portuguese)
straat (Dutch)

map (English)
carte (French)
mapa (Spanish)
Stadtplan (German)
carta geografica (Italian)
mapa (Portuguese)
kaart (Dutch)

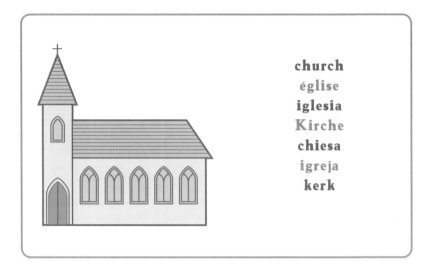

church
église
iglesia
Kirche
chiesa
igreja
kerk

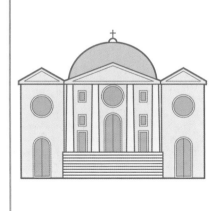

cathedral
cathédrale
catedral
Kathedrale
cattedrale
catedral
kathedraal

art gallery
musée d'art
galería d'arte
Kunstgalerie
galleria d'arte
galeria d'arte
kunstgalerie

museum
musée
museo
Museum
museo
museu
museum

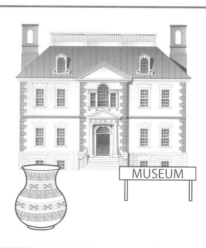

excursions
excursions
excursiones
Exkursionen
gita
excursão
excursies

tour guide
guide d'excursion
guía turístico
Tourführer
guida di turismo
guia de excursão
reisgids

audio guide
audio-guide
audio-guía
Audioführer
guida audio
guia audio
audiorondleiding

walking tour
excursion de marche
viaje que camina
Wanderung
escursione a piedi
excursão passear
wandelreis

tourist information
tourist bureau
oficina de turismo
Fremdenverkehrsamt
ufficio turistico
posto de turismo
VVV

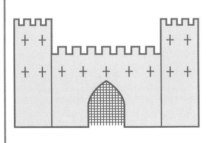

castle
château
castillo
Schloß
castello
castelo
kasteel

gardens
jardins
jardines
Gärten
giardini
jardins
tuinen

park
parc
parque
Park
parco
parque
park

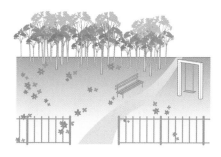

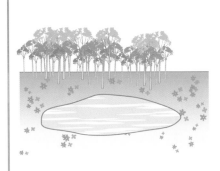

lake
lac
lago
See
lago
lago
meer

temple
temple
templo
Tempel
tempia
tempio
tempel

market
marché
mercado
Markt
mercato
mercado
markt

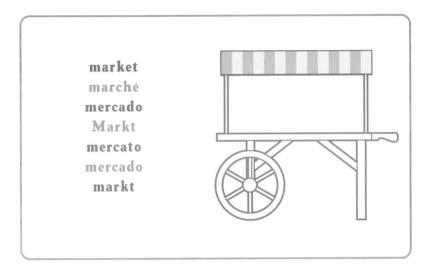

monument
monument
monumento
Denkmal
monumento
monumento
monument

palace
palais
palacio
Palast
palazzo
palácio
paleis

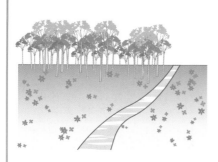

river
rivière
río
Fluß
fiume
rio
rivier

tower
tour
torre
Turm
torretta
torre
toren

camera
appareil-photo
cámara fotográfica
Kamera
macchina fotografica
máquina fotográfica
fototoestel

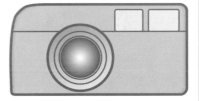

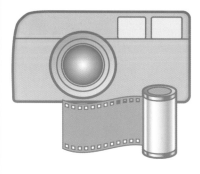

photography
photographie
fotografía
Fotografie
fotografia
fotografia
fotografie

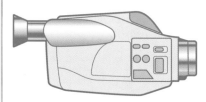

camcorder
caméscope
cámara de vídeo
Videokamera
videocamera
câmara vídeo
videocamera

zoo
zoo
zoológico
Zoo
zoo
jardim zoológico
dierentuin

statue
statue
estatua
Statue
statua
estátua
standbeeld

Numbers

one, two, three, four, five, six, seven, eight, nine, ten, eleven, twelve, thirteen, fourteen, fifteen, sixteen, seventeen, eighteen, nineteen, twenty, thirty, fourty, eighty, ninety, one hundred, thousand, million, billion, trillion, one, two, three, four, five, six, seven, eight, nine, ten, eleven, twelve

5 five, cinq, cinco, fünf, cinque, cinco, vijf

6 six, six, seises, sechs, sei, seis, zes

7 seven, sept, siete, sieben, sette, sete, zeven

8 eight, huit, ocho, acht, otto, oito, acht

9 nine, neuf, nueve, neun, nove, nove, negen

10 ten, dix, diez, zehn, dieci, dez, tien

11 eleven, onze, once, elf, undici, onze, elf

12 twelve, douze, doce, zwölf, dodici, doze, twaalf

13 thirteen, treize, trece, dreizehn, tredici, treze, dertien

1 one, un, uno, ein, uno, um, één

2 two, deux, dos, zwei, due, dois, twee

3 three, trois, tres, drei, tre, três, drie

4 four, quatre, cuatro, vier, quattro, quatro, vier

14 fourteen, quatorze, catorce, vierzehn, **quattordici**, quatorze, **veertien**

15 fifteen, quinze, quince, fünfzehn, **quindici**, quinze, **vijftien**

16 sixteen, seize, dieciséis, sechzehn, **sedici**, dezesseis zestien

17 seventeen, dix-sept, diecisiete, siebzehn, **diciassette**, dezessete, **zeventien**

18 eighteen, dix-huit, **dieciocho**, achtzehn, **diciotto**, dezoito, **achttien**

19 nineteen, dix-neuf, diecinueve, neunzehn, **diciannove**, dezenove, **negentien**

20 twenty, vingt, **veinte**, Zwanzig, **venti**, vinte, **twintig**

30 thirty, trente, treinta, dreißig, **trenta**, trinta, **dertig**

40 forty, quarante, cuarenta, vierzig, **quaranta**, quarenta, **veertig**

50 fifty, cinquante, **cincuenta**, fünfzig, **cinquanta**, cinqüenta, **vijftig**

60 sixty, soixante, **sesenta**, sechzig, **sessanta**, sessenta, **zestig**

70 seventy, soixante-dix, **setenta**, siebzig, **settanta**, setenta, **zeventig**

80 eighty, quatre-vingts, **ochenta**, achtzig, **ottanta**, oitenta, **tachtig**

90 ninety, quatre-vingt-dix, **noventa**, neunzig, **novanta**, noventa, **negentig**

100 hundred, cent, ciento, hundert, **cento**, cem, **honderd**

1,000 thousand, mille, **mil**, tausend, **mille**, mil, **duizend**

1,000,000 million, million, **millón**, Million, milione, milhão, **miljoen**

Index